This publication is made possible by the support of the Indiana Arts Commission, the National Endowment for the Arts, the Vanderburgh Community Foundation, the University of Southern Indiana College of Liberal Arts, the USI Foundation, and the USI Society for Arts & Humanities.

Skin

Music

For Larry Ray Van Horn

Contents

†

†

†

†

†

†

Give me love or electrocution...lots

–Chris Whitley, "Altitude"

Variations on the Death by Drowning of the Poet, Paul Celan

The heart in drowning must not be luminous

star-lit

but some porous leaf shape
knifing the current

unaltered and
unappeased

the *I* in the mind's arch casting its one last vowel

and then in that other syntax

(the river's surface) not even this

wave troughs: cross-beamed/spectral—

a numb fluttering

as death opens

a fin-shape in the bottom's flank

†

Still things accost him—

the night with its invisible reefs

and now the day too

all of it reflecting river/beautiful glass

the spray of larks

etching in the new bud's matrix

a spray of larks

and him speckled too in a new skin

a spiral of flesh the reeds finger

        meadow-ward/seaward

      †

What nourishes his heart now

       what sleeps with light in the iris

in honor of urns
    and thresholds

hidden threads embrace him

      (now it is raining
       in all the rooms)

tree limbs chisel and mar

      the drum made of coarse grass

and pubic hair

still alive in the distance

     thumbed   diminished

over open ground

      †

     Can a tree shiver and take his place

can obsession reign   the river — a slit
vein/a silt

vein — reinvents itself in language

      thewordmade
      fleshmadeash
      madesnow

that something hidden

                                     rudderless

still rasping beside him

picked up/tumbled

                                     cutting his hands

from the reeds/the evening/everything

†

Now a folding occurs that takes his breath away

                                     an explosion of
                                     black stars

wanting less and less of the narrative

                                   the shard-splintered wreckage

the ecstasy unbearable

                                 cooked gold

the dead lay easily in his hands

tooth-bits   tresses of light   the coiled eyes of snails

†

Elsewhere, air gushes more sharp-tongued than grief

                                   cranial and
                                   wholly mad

in the dahlia hollows

the deathframe windowless

                                   shadowless

clear shallow water   breadth of the broad canal

song of tireblade with corona

the nulling tricks of the ear   soft ripples

                                        flattening this slant
                            decay

                    †

Cool sink of the circular night

                            his place pinned down

with star points   and daggering ether

silk leaves winded
to nothingness

he drifts in the calving light

                                        ungrounded
                            still to be found

and chirrs astonishment

as if this cut in gravity
                        this blood Sabbath
were the only refuge

                self-blessing clenched in a water-skinned fist

WHITE HEAT

My mother stands before the white heat, but for her
it is more Cagney

than Dickinson, sweat
pants

and a tray of pills, cable, that good son
on a tower of fuel

calling out to his ma.
I'm all undercover,

unanointed,
Edmund O'Brien working his prison con.

For her part, she can recall the exact evening
in 1949

when she first saw the film,
what she wore, what she ate, what the air was like

on the walk home.
The camera swings—

she waves a bruised arm, points
at Virginia Mayo,

B actress, moll,
shouts, *Danny Kaye — Walter Mitty.*

Pulls her top down
just enough

to reveal where the quivering substance plays.
Little anvil,

hammer poised to jolt her heart
should that muscle fail.

It's a good
scar

she runs her fingertip into, a zippered Braille.
And then the movie

ends. The mother's dead,
the son ignited,

a rush of memory
and piano.

All those schoolgirl lessons coming back
in the curve of

her hands, the shape
of her back—

1947, '52, the difficult
labor, how

my living almost killed her. She
plays. I

listen. The hammers'
finer forge refines the melody—a pile of din and flame.

OKINAWA DOG

Black dog, black wave,
his little Okinawa,
you don't eat for days and
so he cries Odysseus tears,
faces of the dead coming
back to him in paw
and greased pelt—
your eyes gone skyward—
soldier chewed
by bullet and sand.
And so the laying out
of memory in the body
of a dog, the needle
to the leg. I know
it is not easy dying,
or watching his nerves
fly through rings of time
so it is almost the arc
of planets he impales
with each hesitant step.
Mercury huge (his daughter says)
because the sky is so clear.
Wife's body shelved,
a box of ashes. Perpetual
weaving. The Florida sun
her only suitor.
There is a bed, I know, carved
from the heart of a tree,
but he does not sleep
there. Dogless, he paces.
Dogless, because a new one
will pull him down. He'll
fall, I suspect, when that time
comes, willingly.
But for now, his box
of stills. The pith helmet.

Pre-invasion breakfast
of steak and eggs.
That one photo we lingered
over when we first met —
a Japanese soldier, a boy,
with his right big toe
crammed into the trigger
guard, rifle barrel pressed to
the chin. Cold penny
of death, back of his head
glued to the sand. We
stared at it a long time
before he turned it over
and — because you were still
alive — petted your neck,
rambled off a buddy's
name...Then, not one tear.

ICE: PRELUDES TO A MEMORY OF HEAVEN

Again, the kingdom of heaven is like unto a merchant man, seeking goodly pearls...

Matthew 13:45

In the dream, bitter cold. Two men
sawing

at ice
until large chunks can be lifted,

carried to a flatbed truck, laid on straw.

Again
and again down the incline,

their breath white against the snow.

Then up again,
building

a kind of house.

It takes hours to do this. Their hands are bare.
Snow not deep,

but slick,
so they step carefully.

The dream-shot has me as bird or tree,
so I cannot see

the meat of their faces,

but they seem —
since this is my waking reference —

to be penniless.
The lake is a kingdom and so they harvest,

until the bed is full
and

they climb in,
drive away.

†

Second dream — same lake —

different men.

There's a pickup backed to the ice,
and they are tugging,

positioning the weight of an animal
at the lip

of the gate
until they can haul it

twenty feet out.

It hangs between them like something drowned,
or sleeping.

And then they drop it —

a doe hunted down or roadkill,
the dream won't say.

And then they are
gone.

The body steams a little in the cold.

The men park on a hill
overlooking the surface,

watch eagles
one by one

unlock themselves from the hammered sky,
flutter

in,
tear and feed.

†

I know the structure cannot hold

but as long as it does
it is sheened.

The straw soaked through —
a drowned man's hair.

The impossible gem melting down —

striations
that for awhile resemble knives,

bleeding pearls.

As for the deer, it is scraped
to bone.

Emptiness where the eyes were set.

Ribs still holding
their curve.

Skeleton—target of fur and blood
gone feathery at the edges,

until it is dragged away
in pieces,

or drops,
unhinged,

through water returned to water.

St. Catherine's Head Through Binoculars

Because the lighting shifts, she's crescent at first,
then waxed, waning,

brutally
gibbous.

Spent fuel rod
in the church of our Lord,

San Domenico, Siena.
The head smuggled out of Rome in a sack,

converted by miracle to rose petals when a guard
peered in.

Now at the core a boxed intelligence.
Ropes and bars

to keep us away.
Though someone is shooting photos

against the law
of the church

and is shamed back to the wedge of silence
by a boy

who has been scraping from the votive trough
day-old wax

the consistency
of Catherine's face.

And so I draw her upside down as Galileo did the moon,
her saintliness

rendered in horns of light
and crackleware.

Oceanus Procellarum:
ocean of storms in pencil and smudge.

Her gaze
rising out of the scratchings.

It's a crude face,
this godliness.

A crude science.
To which I don't kneel and don't pay, but light a candle.

FLOOD

Cedar Rapids, Iowa, 2008

Shook foil—that's what a river is. Catfish hauled like bars
of iron

from a midtown bridge,
the wire that holds them

so flexed with twisting it bleeds a mercury back
to the water

the exact length of childhood:
gradient through Butler County, Black Hawk,

Linn.
Now, early third millennium,

the Cedar rages all night from the north
(less crushed oil

than river sludge,
all the down-sloping streets'

hammering runoff).
The city,

a ruined Venice.
My mother weeps at all the gilded damage.

The ornate Paramount,
the Court House rising—white stone island

on its island
now buried, middle of the river

until the city is regrained,
remapped,

fractured, grafted,
a 1937 bus ride

cut
with nickel candy, early 60s/

cut/
my brother standing one block off the river

one week post-flood
a full head below the high-water line.

If YouTube is the way we mourn,
if soundtrack, if

Creed,
then I am a boy again in a Chevy

cruising that curve
past Quaker Oats

and the factory where my father worked,
past the hospital

where I was born,
air

full of greening summer
and secondhand smoke,

the beautiful scarf
of adulthood alive in the scent of beer,

ball of tar
warm in the hand like a just-birthed heart...

Ah, Atlantis—
already I'm forgetting your raw papyrus

to be written on
dries months later

(the houses still rotting)
when I drive your streets to this ghettoed dirt.

Skin Music: A Memoir

After forty years I still wonder about the carp and our neighbor. Whatever possessed him to spend all that time catching a creel's-worth of bottom feeders, cleaning, filleting, breading, deep-frying, then walking down the alley in time for *our* dinner, saying he'd cooked us some catfish?

    We often ate catfish we caught from the river so it seemed right.

> It was a gift, summer's
> > bounty, the plate
> something

> > he'd fashioned
> from crimped
> > aluminum foil...

And so we said our thanks and ate, completing the joke.

    I will never understand it. Was it a dig at my father—his subtle arrogance—despite four kids and a lousy job? Were they drinking buddies? My father took his accordion up there sometimes and played unhinged polkas on Saturday nights.

    I think now his point was Shakespearean, vicious. The man's cruel knowledge, our blindness, that he was eating the neighborhood children.

    The carp was their flesh.

†

    In retrospect the strategies were astounding. For the adults first— *win their hearts*—the man built a horseshoe pit and badminton court in the schoolyard across the alley.

> Long into dusk the shuttlecock
> > whirred, the horseshoes
> clanged and spun.

    Afterwards, gin and tonics, cigarettes, laughter, talk, 8 mm cartoons he sometimes ran backwards.

In the yard, a set of bars, high and low, a child could hang from, arms stretched out, pure orangutan,

> or swing from the knees,
> > sundress sailing.

And then in a stroke of brilliance on that twenty x forty lot he buried coffee cans for miniature golf, all eighteen holes, front to back.

He even let the children paint the side of his house with water. Hours they spent brushing in sunlight, letting it dry, repainting in long strokes what seemed a jungle—the house was green.

This was hunting season, exquisite patience.

> The days unwinding, heating
> > up,
> > the hedges coming apart

as a lone child appeared.

†

It comes out later that you want to kill somebody who's already dead—

> a brother's seventeen, still wetting
> > the sheets, it's
> > a sister's wedding day—and

then suddenly you're in a car with baseball bats and hammers heading for that old block.

Your grandfather wants to drive a nine-inch nail into the man's heart, but the man's dead so you just circle, up D Avenue shouting his name, and then down the alley, back again.

Thinking what next.

Thinking how brazen the bastard was, lazy in a way, disciplined—
it was his own block—

whispering some germ of fear,
self-poison, into
a child's ear before

he pulled the kid's pants down.

That secret voice, part man, part boy or girl, like wet shoelace, double-looped, frozen.

No matter how you move, alone, in another's arms, it won't unknot.

†

Nine or ten at the time, I was too old for him.

I owned jackknives, pubic hair, a fishing pole.

Had an arch enemy the next house over, Carroll Stephen Luckey the III—how perfect was that—we, the Blakeslee boys and I, tried to drown once and who later shot at us from his roof with a pellet gun because we teased him when he cleaned his hamster cage and stuffed the two creatures like a pair of mittens into a Mason jar—to protect them— then closed the lid...

We had hydrochloric acid,
wrist rockets we'd
built from hangers,

Schwinn bikes. Every dime we begged or stole

we'd spend on candy, Ohio
Blue Tips, then
ride to the slough,

try to set ourselves, the world, on fire.

Zipper, stretched jeans, dirty nail, it didn't matter.

We were covered in scabs, waved to the child molester as we angled past him, perfect in our bodies, throwing stones, cussing, on our way to the movies burning with other idle men.

†

And then it was night.
Temperature and wind overlaid the scattered pools of human skin
until it was one water ghosting the alley.

Carroll Stephen Luckey the II
finally able
to screw his wife, now

his son was sleeping, and those rude boys who earlier had thrown dirt
clods against his upstairs window as he tried slowly to disrobe her—

beautiful,
lovely
shadow play—

had gone home to their nightly beatings.
The youngest children asleep in their pods of covers, post-invasion,
bodies snatched, building sad alien selves.
The child molester wide awake two houses over in a second-storey
room,

terrified of winter
and
empty yards.

His body as still as the elaborate train set he'd built in his basement.
Dust settling everywhere.
On the families disembarking, the delicate signs, the false eye of
the engine.

†

I saw my first naked girl
that year,
a Blakeslee daughter.

The boys had drilled holes in the plywood wall between the bedrooms so when she showered that June day we raced ahead and waited for her to dress.

Three eyes to three holes, two brothers, neighbor, all idiots, the girl stretching, unaware, like Athena in the mirror.

I remember the whiteness of her belly,

> the just-budding nipples,
> faint,
> pink, and

> was lost in how quiet
> her
> gaze was. My own gaze

part skin, part music, reefing a shore I could barely imagine.

And then the spell broke.

She dressed and was dork girl again, sheathed in innocence.

Numbed, altered, torqued, I looked for my bike, loaded pole and matches, lures and bait, headed for the creek.

> It was summer, always high
> summer,
> in that blistered world.

I caught fish.

Old enough to get fucked in the ass, or suck a derelict's dick, I thought of that girl immaculate before the mirror, then put my knife to the gill.

CARAVAGGIO'S *MEDUSA* AS A BOX OF NAILS

Forty pounds of iron/brass/wood screws
lag bolts/nuts/picture wire
this was the aluminum milk box my father used
to keep his refuse hardware in
Home Town Dairy filled to the brim
I had to push it a corner at a time
twenty dollars at a time
to get it from under the bench
so I could palm its spiky crown
it was useless treasure to me
all the things a man never builds
solidified by gravity
to one nuclear core
more tomb debris than new circuits
drywall shimmering like panels of milk
a hundred times I set my hand down
to lift a portion of that writhing head
my gaze pushed into polished concrete
itself a mirror reflecting my twisted face
shoulder/mound of bicep
veined and pumped
who would turn to stone then
sister ratting another doll's head with match
and comb
mother singing to baby brother/baby blue
diaper pin

dangling from her mouth like a cigarette

neighbor kid in the next yard

with a Tommy gun

doing his best Vic Morrow belly crawl

Vietnam

not even a cool silk jacket yet

a fading dragon tattoo

father finally down from the roof

punctured/shingling

gone/and back/alone

shoulder sore from where they gave him the tetanus

six pack under his arm

or just me

that handful of nails I managed to lift

like a possible future

little Gorgon's face reflected

in bubbled aluminum

her astonishment at her own terrifying glance

like the birth of death and bone

I held the package tight

in the damp spring air

brought it down like a reckless hammer

nail to nail/screw to screw

building something bloodied/muscled

then stepped across the threshold

and climbed high in the apple

as winged as Pegasus with blossom

RADIUM CITY

It was the watches I wanted, those radium dials
glowing like bombsights

when I cupped my palm.
Wisp

of radioactivity—the hour hand;
nether-wisp—the second.

For weeks my mother worked the counter at Kresge's—
her faded pink smock

as tight as a nurse's—
as she laid out the bands in their false

reptilian shines—
the cowboy tans, the avocado greens. This

was Radium City
and my mother, Marie

Curie, scientist of jewels and hams,
the chunks of meat slapped

into the knife and the iridescence sliced
to pieces thin

as winter sky, shaved uranium.
I had to stack them high to tongue the plugs

of fats, the permeating salts.
The roll breaking in my hands like a ball of

glass. And the stench of drugstore
popcorn, its second perfume

mingling with what my mother wore
as she shoveled out

bags like spent carnival fortunes.
More money was one we wasted on ourselves.

Or new drapes.
One last snap of the Tupperware over the nightly concoctions

no one ever wanted to eat.
I'd go away and ponder mono/stereo

for the extra buck
in the LP bins, or keep an eye walking

home for Tarzan—
Weissmuller in a shiny Olds or Cadillac.

And then wait out the summer hours pitching
a nine-inning game

into a chalk box on the side of the house.
Ferguson Jenkins for seven or so,

then Abernathy for the submarine.
Next door a neighbor would peg out his pet

skunk and I'd listen as it roiled
with thirst

or hunkered under diving blue jays,
their cobalts dipped

in the mouth of the sun.
The Cubs would lose.

Weissmuller never show.
The Mexican kids from Dempster would threaten

to beat my ass into the street
and leave me there

dented and ringing as a hubcap,
another rat-faced kid

waiting for his mother to come home.
Pink smock.

Ham in a pocket.
Singing beyond the genius of the meats.

The kiss,
the mother's kiss, put like a cure to the child's face.

MY BUCEPHALUS,

my cloud shape, my incidental, somewhere
                    there is a child
            standing in dirt,

shitting its ankles, but you are
                    running
            again in that Canadian field, tight

along the fence rail,
                    so that your speed
            matches mine

and it is not the speed of an old woman
                    swatting
            flies from an open

cut, or the move (since I am well-fed)
                    from wound
            to blossom

to wound and I am birthed again
                    in sunlight,
            freed from my shadow.

Your pinto high-step whispers,
                    your proud
            pounding

for no good reason. The bold tower
                    of losses
            that on earth

conveys our misery just one more silo
                    of grain
            in an Ontario field.

And still you run. Over the fence rail,
                    around the curve,
          and back

again where you bed down
                    and whinny,
          roll

on your back. I have seen you there,
                    pointing
          belly at sky,

all that shining muscular roundness.
                    I have seen
          the crisp,

rudimentary hooves.
                    Where was I
          going that was so important

that I could not stop
                    and place a hand
          on your broad,

flat skull, consider your huge
                    eyes—
          not all broken glass,

pieces of cloud, but
                    jeweled, encompassed,
          as if packed with stone.

Somewhere a man imagines
                    his wife's
          cancer as small islands forever

leaving her body. While elsewhere
                    bullets
          fragment, go

butt-headed, twin-pronged,
             rip
        flesh. And still you run, so far

to the edge of the field,
             it is memory,
        horizon,

and I am walking to the fence,
             my body
        the consistency

of balsa and myth,
             the angle of my leaning
        like a lure

to heaven. I wonder: When I finally
             see
        the god face, will it be you, a horse?

BAPTISM

I held my breath a long time before I let the drowning take over.
And then I was stood up, was put upon.

Larynx like a great cup wrapped in muscle
held to the light.

Jesus yip and howl.
Pre-Janis, pre-James Brown.

More pop than anything.
Beatle-esque, Mersey Beat.

The preacher's hands still snorkeling my mouth.
White gown heavy and gelatinous with holy tap water.

It would take a long time before the howl
would cure

into something rawer, more sexual.
Wilson Picket's midnight hour, Sam and Dave,

The Four Tops.
Moonlight gloving my white boy's hands

like a beautiful suede
as I pawed

whomever I was with back then
in the back of my father's aqua Mustang

and got pawed back.
The organs of voice and respiration—

the catamaran of the lungs
when we curled up and pretended to sleep,

the mediastina,
the cargoed hearts—

dormant for awhile in the mystery of skin
and Jesus

until the hermit (whose land this was, this back road)
crashed through the trees.

In her face lit by dash light I saw the moon
of my becoming

take its second shape as I fishtailed out
of a pile of spitting gravel,

hermit with a shotgun like a cross-beam
and a pumping fist.

We'd stolen something from him we couldn't name
and so we hit the highway.

Sucked our breath.
Radio-offed his rage.

She lifted her head to laugh, revealed for an instant
her muscular throat.

Scent of her skin on my skin,
I brought my fingers to my face

and let the coolness breathe.
Then rocked the car into the valley of her singing.

DIALYSIS

Blood wants an angel but all it has is Monday,
my mother

three states away,
left arm snaked and buttonholed

for dialysis.
What do they dream—mother

and blood—those long hours
churning?

Permeable membrane
there same as here: potassium expelled, magnesium,

wreckage of husband,
father.

What is collected: reverse Eden
in a jar.

Just five seconds ago I batted away a honey bee.
Now it's back,

my kneecap sweet
as rhododendron.

The bee's flight: long trail of zigging then on a rope
to the hive,

its news: *nectar everywhere*.
My mother purrs, I

purr in a drift
of consciousness—

blood spurting
in packets the size of a bee

or hanging
in those death-red capillarial nets—human torsos—

I saw once
polymered to nothingness.

We breathe, the ribs
expand,

the living lungs inflate.
That perverse museum—

she's going to die,
I'll have to watch—

like so much shaken pollen
I'll need a trowel as wide as my hand

to get one clear cylinder of gold,
that thicket

of wild flower—her glory days—
soon coating my throat.

Throat wants to say something,
blood and honey,

it always does,
but it's dead air now

inside the daylight.
Heat crowning scalp, bees in the yard

like weed fluff,
bands of silence.

Mother leaning back, idling,
but still pegged down.

Bees for an instant
hovering in the shape of a mouth.

TRAIN STOPPED ALONG AN EMBANKMENT

If time everlasting is the final gesture
and we, sometimes without our bodies,

its careless servant,
then darkness will be its own good end,

and the cooling down
a thing vital to the next shift in matter.

But for now we wait.
The train

on its high throne along the countryside.
Smell of

creosote from the roadbed. Dying
fish. The whole string of them

where the boy fell like the imperfect fossil
of his luck—

dragged twice across the grading
because the first man there

leaned down as if to retrieve them,
then thought better of his fate—

such
smears of autumn daylight—train

crew and rescue workers up and down
the right-of-way, authority not yet

done with the scene.
And so one reads, or charts, the breakdown

of the stellar fires, while another spoons
yogurt into her daughter's mouth;

another on a cell phone crying *here*
and *lateness*—

who can really say what the body feels
in going down that

hard, the whoosh almost killing
first—*neck hairs rising,*

arm hairs rising—before the lightning strike
of mass, the train even now,

stalled,
a fanged, forward aching,

its spectral light at the tip of speed
what dying starlight tells us.

Though you could walk back down
the triple length of

cars and watch the pitched cruisers
strobe the whole day red

through which the crowd dispersed
and leaves

fell—some like galaxies
or moths that could spot both hands

with intricate, flammable wing thrusts;
others like birds

who dive, reckless, full-
throttled, into the creek's black water.

EVERY CORAL BRANCH SUPPORTS THE MOON

Answer to a Zen koan (for my mother)

There was a river in her head that kept flowing
and so she

sang
at a piano built

from air,

hands
frail and spotted with match heads.

Strange singer she was,

mask
forcing pressure

into a failing heart
so the external lung that kept pumping

was nearly opera

in the room, grand, scaled—
La Scala—

and the chambers of her dying

its box
and voice.

But no sound came. Plank
on plank

she kept building,

reaching out,
leaning,

bridging some lumber in her head

with deeper wood.
I thought fear

would take her
like some Jesus bucket

tearing

at the bottom of a well
when the preacher

gripped her skull

and uttered last harsh words,
but it was she

who came to drink,
not some savior

in the shape

of a man's palm.
And so I too sucked breath

in hospital light,

brought her dripping
from the sea.

Gave her a *cup of winter*,
language

having clotted in a sheath of thought—

a particle
of ice—

it was all she could whisper,

dying,
to get a glass of cooling tea...

Reader,
it was morphine.

I let them wand her heart

to disconnect it,
and then we pumped the slurry in.

Nobody winced

because it was beautiful and smooth,
a fat,

controllable lightning,
cured

with honey.

How it serenely sleeved the wires of her brain,
the nerves,

the cheekbones I saw yellowed

with jaundice,
that Taj Mahal of heresy and belief

we call the self
come crashing down,

zone

by zone, reduced, relaxed,
surrendered

to one thin hand caressing a cold dead leg.

Fragment: Winter Journal

...then seizure again, that
blue clot, level

of the larynx,
can't breathe, can't

speak, don't want to,
heron long gone

(where?), no longer
perfecting its one

slant move: *stillness*
stabbing at shadow,

its throat (no cry)
muscle of fin

and writhing, all
I dream

is blue weather,
blue snow

on a blue roof,
Rilke's zombie angels

fixed in this world
for now, sharp,

angular ice,
halfway down the river

the trees are dirty with them,
as bent as

fishhooks, sundown:
last red wash of emptiness,

last seizure, ice cracking,
then seizure again...

Boom Boom

It's a shit deal, death, so we play
cards. Pinochle, two of
everything—ace, ten, king, the
neutered nine, dog's tail
whacking the open sore on his
knee, big toe bandaged as if
already amputated. He bluffs
for the bid, drops a card, says he
can't bend. I offer a ridiculous
I know. He spits back
a *no you don't* so quick to clarify
the borders I can only offer
a second, more ridiculous *I know*,
meaning this time *I don't*. It's
him feeling nothing below the
knees, his hands to follow, death
by saliva to follow, the brain-
body engine working on frayed
string strung so far into an empty
sky, the kite (his body)
is an ungovernable weight, his
mind (the string) a limp thing
in his hands. Tug, and nothing
happens. Lyric says *sail on, sail
on*, bitch siren naked on a wet
rock, slung song and foam.
Meanwhile, down here, wind
side, it takes him three tries to
stand, the thought *just get up*
ringing like a penny in a tin can,
so long he soils himself. For
an instant I see him naked at the
doorway, washrag at his
belly, a shamed Adam. Later,
last hand, I forget the second
ace, stupid me, there are two of

everything: our eyes, our hands,
our thumbs, our scrotums, split
fruit of the brain, dignity. He
beats me by five points, the ex-
Marine, I think he likes me. I'm
a quick study, wiseass, good with
old men. I value their stupidities
and blindness, the poetry (*sail
on*) of their ordinary lives. Add
it to my own stupidity and
blindness. The art of pinochle now.
Bitching, not bitching, poisoning
rats, getting laid, dreaming,
playing guitar. Everything in sevenths,
key of E, glass slide. If I start now
and play the 100,000 songs built
on this one progression, I'll John
Lee Hooker my own dirt path
through his Parkinson's (*boom
boom boom boom, it's gonna
shoot him right down*), through
my mother's ruined kidneys, churn
and wash, tumor and scarred lungs
of friends, all this fretwork to a boot
worn down to sock, coin of bone and
(the strings will insist on this, they
too conjure a siren body, siren mind,
foam and rock) two broken hands.

SOCKET AND DRILL

Woodpecker, far tree. The
bark sounds soft from this
distance and so I turn the
television low to better hear
the pause and stab. In
the gap, seed birds
like pockets of antimatter.
Is it territory or pleasure
they work? I can't say.
Sounds flash electric in
curtains of air.
Woodpecker silent now,
pulled back into dark
matter. Clouds still gray.
Round sun sailing lost in
its socket. And then just
as suddenly, it is Tuesday,
high summer. A spider
overnight has dropped a
web as fine as sugar
between the clothesline and
Adirondack chair. It sways
in the wind—Tibetan,
fractal. Drumhead, trap,
net of prayer. Still I hang
my clothes—black shirt,
shorts, wheel of nothingness,
faded pants. Two blocks
over, the churned river pours
through a gate in the dam
like a fabulous drill.
The siren warning cuts
through a hundred
thousand leaves, across
roofs, and into my neighbor's
garden. The gate

widening. More gravity
racing through. Fishermen
are up to their hips in it, their
lines almost tender
in the murk. If mercy is here,
if salvation, it is not
in these ghost strands,
my wife's torso
hung out as drying,
matted linen. It is not
in the woodpecker, worms,
stink of bait, the purgatorial,
wind-pushed, dried-up morsels
of hope that crawl
forever in our heads, the river's
dream of passage, our
passage—*drip*—like a catechism—
the sounding into
our ears—*drip*. Spider's
body and silk reduced—because
I destroy it—to ruined silver.

DROWN

Fraudulent river, how can
I believe anything you
say? I walk past nine trees, see
a bird, and then that one man
fishing at the edge of vi-
sion is floating by. I can't
see the body at first so
I think his waders are the
trousers of the Lord swelled with
runoff and velocity
from the dam. But they are not.
I don't wade in. The others
with me don't wade in. We just
stroll along, watch the trousers
betray the current through a
flock of un-nerved ducks. It is
only when I call to the
fishermen paddling by to
touch a heel and they recoil
that I sense the heaviness
you carry. Fat man on a
graying Sunday dead of a
busted vein or bubble
in the heart so his body
caved and his garments filled and
he was flannelled thrashing in
waist-deep water. Somebody
must have called from the dam, then
leaned back, fishing. Smoked above
the whirlpools and raw-toothed flail-
ing until the river was
gentle and flat. I am on
the bridge when they pull him out,
so much spilling from his face
I think he is the source of
molten silver. Eyes wide o-

pen. Packed with stone. Because that's
what you are, river, stone lung
and stone heart they try to beat
to life again with useless
hands. Body hauled—such import-
ant fury—from a yellow
rubber boat to the anvil
of a rotted dock, I think
a living blade might be forged
fist by fist. My fist if I'd
waded in. My lips two sparks
to ignite a cough. Or what-
ever that stutter is when
the dying gasp and fountain
unrepentant river to
the streaming earth. I wait. No
such breath forthcomes. No such birth.
Just spidery rush-off—ech-
o of a man. How can I
believe anything it says?

LANDSCAPE WITH DESERT AND RIVER

New ice hangs from the roof of itself
        and spikes
    down—glacial, toothed—into the riverbed.

The riverbank: a Franz Kline gestating—bar
        of black,
    field of white—and then that angular

crosshatching. As if there were a form
        big enough
    to contain the world. As if

the name were the name. I walk
        a long time
    as ice thickens, as cold drives

blood from my hands.
        Where does it go—
    the blood? How far backwards like vision

into the heart? I have lived thirty years
        beside this river's coiling,
    its rough shot over

and under dams. Its bitter whiskey
        must have
    some purchase, must spin some torqued thread

of sediment...

        †

        Or perhaps it is just glass,
    the way my ankles felt

coming down the alluvial fan, up
                    each step
          the shape of water, a little erosion,

each skull-sized rock pushing back,
                    then down
          the same,

as darkness silted in, Death Valley,
                    Christmas,
          its metamorphic volume.

I could feel heat slipping its radiance
                    as easily
          as skin, and knew my own skin would

follow. All that gold light falling down,
                    crowning the dunes,
          all that last blue,

imperial, swelling to black. And then that rush
                    to the bottom,
          the cold grasses

like stacks of hay. We gasped, breathless—
                    there, at our feet,
          gone glassy with walking,

a rattler's shed skin, coiled
                    as if to strike us.
          Purity for purity in an impure world,

spiritless flute...

                              †

                    My body in water, my
          body in stone,

what is the bloodless falling into these
                    alternate selves: desert and river?
          I feel both

course through me like wind
                    through the skin of a snake,
          shining nerve of

nothingness. I feel the crippling touch
                    of dusk,
    Scudera hatching in the west,

its grand square of blue, last painting,
                    like a window
          to the gods shutting down, something

red escaping. River: still sheet ice.
                    No birds walking.
          Tongue of the sublime, my tongue, cloaking

it all with language. A perfect circle
                    in the skull,
          sweet sentence: *want*. I want *Scudera*

nailed—bone flag—to every sky. I want
                    to stand in that last
          sun-socket of joy drilling the day,

all raptured up, no rapture,
                    my vintage river
          as immaculate as a tin machine, or desert's dark sister.

HERON

Twice this has happened: I'm driving west into the evening's monochromes
when out of the marshes

> a blue heron struggles
> across
> the highway's five lanes,

so low it nearly hits me, makes me swerve.
        The semi hauling ass behind me slamming its brakes, the cab
dipping, all that forward-driven mass of the trailer

> buffaloing up, nearly
> smacking

the bird from the sky.
        And then the daylight streaming—emptiness streaming—
the leveling out of speed.
        On the windshield:

> five or six blisters
> of marsh.

        Home, each time, I touched what remained of the droplets' glycerin,
then watched them bleed:

> kinked strings picking up
road grit. Husks of rain.

Burn Ward

What did I know then of the resurrection through
metal?

All I saw was how fire had eaten the honey
of his flesh.

Up one leg and into a shoulder,
most of a cheek.

And yet he stood, cradled
the rack, eyes

wet, blistered with shock,
as the cage closed

and the cables snickered in.
I thought Michelangelo's

Christ,
cool stone

(orderly at his elbow,
me carrying vials of blood

STAT
to C-Lab).

That seven-storey lift—last shaft of peacefulness
before the searing

sheeted in
and they'd peel

away his clothes, that fine webbing of
synthetic

and arm.
What howls rose then

beyond the heavy swinging doors
of the Burn Ward?

I walked by for weeks,
tried to see

the debridement,
the reverse burning,

water for
fire—the grafting—

the man partially lizard in that clean room.
The nurses' bodies

through the Demerol
like raw angels

dabbing his burning half with a cotton ball
soaked in silver

until
he was chromed and barred.

A kind of xylophone whose primary song
was pain.

Cool stoke of the hammer:
new flesh (howl),

dream of wife's body, island
he could sink his whole mouth onto,

healed (howl), risen
(howl again)—

time like an anvil—
somebody's face (mine often)

pressed one side of a page-sized window
scratched by breath and hand.

MINOTAUR

The first time I ever reeled from my family's stink I was in the basement of
the Paramount Theater, Cedar Rapids, Iowa, taking a piss. My uncle, nineteen,

retarded—
that's what we called it then—was next
to me.

We had just seen a John Wayne film and were heading home.
I was working hard, nine years old, to drill the urinal but could only
manage a pale yellow rope

that splayed
and went feathery
at the end.

Uncle, for his part, was all bull.
Something powerful and amber coming out of the pizzle he held
with both hands.
Eyes glazed, mind elsewhere. At peace with it—

reek of armpit and
groin
like the air

around a farm.
I could smell in it the drench of decaying skin cell, money, failure,
honeyed ear wax, the genetic rubs that contained my mother (but not my
father).
And so I quailed, zippered up:

boy child, idiot
uncle. Minotaur,
blue baby...

Why

†

did they give him up?

Ward of the state at three or four, I can't recall, he took his ruined crown into the world, bone that would not unstitch, and howled himself to sleep.

Did not die at age six, as he was promised.

But lashed out. Survived.

Learned to steal.

I visited him once in that orphan bedlam. I was thirteen and could barely make him out from all the other smells,

the long rooms, high windows,
shades
pulled so tight

they smacked like canvas.

And then I caught that burning Jesus scent, devil in the whiskers of bristled scalp.

Bad breath hovering beneath coagulant cream.

He grinned hard and hugged me as if I were a friend, and we two perfect creatures in a world of flashy men, gorgeous women, and this moment, the touch

that would tag me his,
though I was already his

†

(how could I know that then?): my own stink coming back in rusted jackknife and cut-up bird, crawdad, creek mud,

wedge of sneaker hanging
over
the culvert

I sometimes crawled through the length of a childhood, the tunnel not holding,

until I re-entered this shining
world
all snot

and dripping phlegm, a scabbed child turning

†

blue: "hue of illness and nobility, the rarest color in nature."

Why did they give him up...

(it's easy now—
Nazis, Pearl
Harbor, there was
metal to save,
sugar
to ration, he
was the fourth child/
flesh issued
damaged
from the mother's
genius womb)

†

cell for cell our own body?
        Now age seventy, they have him tethered down, they think he's
crazy, they have the feeding tube sutured in.

His eyes, my mother's eyes, flash
white
above palsied

vocal chords.
        He blinks to remember: the ten or so cars we owned, where we
lived, who was oldest, who kept him in chocolate, how his pa died and his

ma went crazy, half her head shaved off because she fell down the stairs,
then forgot everything, even his name.

                        And those mean dogs that bit us
                                        and

ran away.
              Miami Drive, 2019 D Avenue.
              The house on Bonita...man-child stumbling in the labyrinths of
our play.
              That ring of silence I held my breath in when I was a kid so I
could be as dumb as him

                        just one more useless dodge
                                        to
                              what they always

told me:

                        how when I was born they put
                                        my
                        crooked body in his open arms

and he cooed my name.

SEVEN-SIDED BOX

Organ²/ASLSP (As SLow aS Possible) is a musical piece composed by John Cage; the current organ performance of the piece began in 2001 and is scheduled to have a duration of 639 years, ending in 2640.

It begins as it must with silence—twenty months of it—enough
        time for an elephant
   to birth (which I did not see on television

the other night—but the calves seemed impossibly happy
        as they played—
   each moment, head-butts and high jinks,

flopping down in dirt, cooling mud—
        the lead female shaking
   her tonnage when the camera veered too close—

audio muted—trumpeting

danger)...The organ itself is simple—as if
        they had taken
   the vocal chords

of a whale and set them on a cold floor.
        Two box shapes—
   something framed like a roof between them—

upright pipes. You could set in the space
        an incredibly
   large bird.

Something extinct—

a dodo—or something just for the joke of it—
        a startled
   ostrich. Either way—bird,

whale, African elephant—it is one sustained cry.
                    And then
            another. Each movement,

the span of a human life. Eight
                    movements
            total, one repeated. A seven-sided

box. Lead weights

and battery backup until the organ dies
                    or the money
            dies. Or—who can think that far ahead?

Make your own list here. Begin and end
                    with God,
            China, the Korengal Valley, bad music,

the structure of drought, cartilage released
                    from the bone,
            debt like a ball-peen hammer coming

to us all.

One drenched pelican is about as far as I can think
                    into the future.
            It is not even

a whale's breath into a flurry of squid.
                    It is not even
            the loneliness of a bull elephant bulking up

so he can rut with a cow. That's hope.
                    Something
            to push beyond our deaths. A little

architecture of egg

and sperm in the womb. Word in the ear,
                    mu-
          sic, next chord. In 2004, they added a pipe

to sequence a pair of E's to an A, C, F#.
                    A blind man
          came to hone his senses. Those that could see

to sit in the presence of the notes sustained
                    (perhaps)
          beyond endurance. How long

before you hum along,

or the sound disappears into the sonic fabric?
                    You have to go away
          to make it

come again. Which is just fine. The church
                    is cold.
          The exterior beaten to death—

a discarded tooth of God. And then
                    that chord
          again. Same chord.

The waves shooting

vertically like a stake into the floor of Heaven.
                    It means
          nothing. It means everything.

It is spirit and not spirit. It pulses
                    and modulates
          as stones cool, as pipes

warp, as wind pushes against the wavelength.
                    As our own bodies'
          heat influences the swell.

So it is

not elephant or whale, but rather
                    sparrow,
          wren,

one fat spider sailing in a neglected
                    corner
          on a silken thread. Something (*what?*)

sliding down as in the horror film I watched
                    a piece of
          the other night. Just

killing time.

Hammering nails into that intractable cross.
                    Head, unfocused.
          Feelings, unfocused. Inevitable death...*As SLow*

aS possible, yes—each instant burns
                    and makes
          its noise until

it spins into nothingness. No flash.
                    Fan blade
          in the third-floor

window propelling the house like an invisible boat...

LITTLE HYDRA, LITTLE GARDEN

Ryōan-ji Garden

Two trains meet and for a moment
their horns collide, open
like a great wing in the night—
car parts to the other side of town,
Port Huron-bound train to the east.
And then that fade, collapse.
Worm of absence.
The sound of the river re-inserts
itself. Rush of the outtake vents
pouring heat into the current
so fish can loll above the dam
before they sluice the gate
into hook and meat.
Downstream: turtles, heron stalking
a patch of mud for something
narrow, silver—minnow,
belly of frog. Newborn ducks
punked out and vulnerable.
All of us in linger and float, awaiting
placement. Angle of vision.
Just last month a neighbor pulled a snapper
from my garden two blocks
off the river and walked it back
like the fifteenth stone. Placed it in the weeds
so no one could see it. All
spring I waited for the hatchlings
to birth—like Ryōan-ji Garden.
Three or four pockets of stone
mimicking islands, creation.
Peaceful dragons. Me
high up because I dwarfed them.
I would have carried them all to the river
had they birthed. I would have,
as the sun arced and dirt warmed,

fingered every stone, stealing
enlightenment. But
then the sun arced, and dirt warmed.
Night bled in through summer trees.
What warrior rose then
from the packed earth? That fat god
riding the moment until the moment
passes, burned down again to ash
and teeth. Heron, duck.
Train horn like a memory
of some former happiness
until it happens again and I test
myself against the fiction, that
bright cinema I keep editing. Wife
hunkering close to mute a nightmare.
Cat sipping air through narrowed
pathways. Her weight against my leg
as dense and curved as a turtle's.

Acknowledgments

The author extends appreciation and acknowledgment to the editors of
the following publications in which some of these poems first appeared:

Crab Orchard Review:	"Train Stopped Along an Embankment"
diode:	"Heron"
FIELD:	"Okinawa Dog"
Hunger Mountain:	"Ice: Preludes to a Memory of Heaven"
	"Variations on the Death by Drowning of the Poet, Paul Celan"
inter|rupture:	"Seven-Sided Box" *[print and online]*
Linebreak:	"Baptism"
The Broken Plate:	"*Boom, Boom*"
The Journal:	"Little Hydra, Little Garden"
The Literary Review:	"Drown"
	"*Every Coral Branch Supports the Moon*"
	"Skin Music: A Memoir"
Portland Review:	"Socket and Drill" *[online]*
	"White Heat" *[print and online]*

Scythe:	"Landscape with Desert and River"
	"My Bucephalus,"
	"St. Catherine's Head Through Binoculars"
Solstice:	"Burn Ward"
	"Dialysis"
	"Flood"
	"Fragment: Winter Journal"
	"Radium City"
Third Coast:	"Caravaggio's *Medusa* as a Box of Nails"

"Minotaur" first appeared in *Electrocution, A Partial History*, which won the Rachel Wetzsteon Chapbook Prize from *Map Literary: A Journal of Contemporary Writing and Art*. Thanks to John Parras and Christopher Salerno.

"Caravaggio's *Medusa* as a Box of Nails" also appeared on *Poetry Daily* and in *New Poetry from the Midwest 2014*.

"Drown" also appeared in *Poetry in Michigan/Michigan in Poetry* published by New Issues Press, and in *Electrocution, a Partial History*.

"Flood" also appeared in the print anthology *Selections from Solstice*.

Many thanks to Dorothy Brooks and Cindy Hunter Morgan for friendship, feedback, and support. To the Britten Avenue Crew (Ann Andrews, Joyce Benvenuto, Kate Butler, Sam Mills, Leonora Smith, and Ruelaine Stokes) for the same.

Thanks, too, to Michael Waters and everyone at SIR Press.

NOTES

"Variations on the Death by Drowning of the Poet, Paul Celan"—The body of the poem uses as source code *Poems of Paul Celan* (trans. Michael Hamburger) and *Last Poems* (trans. Katharine Washburn and Margret Guillemin), and briefly, *The Selected Poetry of Rainer Maria Rilke* (trans. by Stephen Mitchell).

"St. Catherine's Head Through Binoculars"—*Sidereus Nuncius* by Galileo.

"Flood"—The opening riffs off "God's Grandeur" by Gerald Manley Hopkins.

"*Every Coral Branch Supports the Moon*"—Title taken from *The Sound of the One Hand: 281 Zen Koans with Answers* (trans. by Yoel Hoffman).

"Minotaur"—The passage quoted is from *The Primary Colors* by Alexander Theroux.

"Little Hydra, Little Garden"—Ryōan-ji Garden contains fifteen rocks arranged on the surface of white pebbles in such a manner that visitors can see only fourteen of them at once, no matter what angle the garden is viewed from. It is said that only when you attain spiritual enlightenment as a result of deep Zen meditation, can you see the last invisible stone.

The Michael Waters Poetry Prize was established in 2013 to honor Michael's contribution to *Southern Indiana Review* and American arts and letters.

MWPP Winners

2014—Dennis Hinrichsen & Hannah Faith Notess
2013—Doug Ramspeck

Southern Indiana Review Press

BOOKS BY DENNIS HINRICHSEN

Electrocution: A Partial History

Rip-tooth

Kurosawa's Dog

Cage of Water

Message to be Spoken into the Left Ear of God

Detail from The Garden of Earthly Delights

The Rain that Falls This Far

The Attraction of Heavenly Bodies